This Client Book Belongs To:

Name: ______________________________

Company: ______________________________

Address: ______________________________

____

License: ______________________________

Log Number: ______________________________

Dates: ______________ to ______________

Phone: ______________________________

Fax: ______________________________

eMail: ______________________________

Website: ______________________________

Facebook: ______________________________

Instagram: ______________________________

Twitter: ______________________________

Other: ______________________________

____

____

Index

Client / Customer	Page

Index

Client / Customer	Page

Index

Client / Customer	Page

Index

Client / Customer	Page

Index

Client / Customer	Page

Client Information

Name:	
Address:	
Phone:	
eMail:	
Notes:	

Date	Time	Service / Work	Price	Notes

Client Information

Name:	
Address:	
Phone:	
eMail:	
Notes:	

Date	Time	Service / Work	Price	Notes

Client Information

Name:	
Address:	
Phone:	
eMail:	
Notes:	

Date	Time	Service / Work	Price	Notes

Client Information

Name:	
Address:	
Phone:	
eMail:	
Notes:	

Date	Time	Service / Work	Price	Notes

Client Information

Name:	
Address:	
Phone:	
eMail:	
Notes:	

Date	Time	Service / Work	Price	Notes

Client Information

Name:	
Address:	
Phone:	
eMail:	
Notes:	

Date	Time	Service / Work	Price	Notes

Client Information

Name:	
Address:	
Phone:	
eMail:	
Notes:	

Date	Time	Service / Work	Price	Notes

Client Information

Name:	
Address:	
Phone:	
eMail:	
Notes:	

Date	Time	Service / Work	Price	Notes

Client Information

Name:	
Address:	
Phone:	
eMail:	
Notes:	

Date	Time	Service / Work	Price	Notes

Client Information

Name:	
Address:	
Phone:	
eMail:	
Notes:	

Date	Time	Service / Work	Price	Notes

Client Information

Name:	
Address:	
Phone:	
eMail:	
Notes:	

Date	Time	Service / Work	Price	Notes

Client Information

Name:	
Address:	
Phone:	
eMail:	
Notes:	

Date	Time	Service / Work	Price	Notes

Client Information

Name:	
Address:	
Phone:	
eMail:	
Notes:	

Date	Time	Service / Work	Price	Notes

Client Information

Name:	
Address:	
Phone:	
eMail:	
Notes:	

Date	Time	Service / Work	Price	Notes

Client Information

Name:	
Address:	
Phone:	
eMail:	
Notes:	

Date	Time	Service / Work	Price	Notes

Client Information

Name:	
Address:	
Phone:	
eMail:	
Notes:	

Date	Time	Service / Work	Price	Notes

Client Information

Name:	
Address:	
Phone:	
eMail:	
Notes:	

Date	Time	Service / Work	Price	Notes

Client Information

Name:	
Address:	
Phone:	
eMail:	
Notes:	

Date	Time	Service / Work	Price	Notes

Client Information

Name:	
Address:	
Phone:	
eMail:	
Notes:	

Date	Time	Service / Work	Price	Notes

Client Information

Name:	
Address:	
Phone:	
eMail:	
Notes:	

Date	Time	Service / Work	Price	Notes

Client Information

Name:	
Address:	
Phone:	
eMail:	
Notes:	

Date	Time	Service / Work	Price	Notes

Client Information

Name:	
Address:	
Phone:	
eMail:	
Notes:	

Date	Time	Service / Work	Price	Notes

Client Information

Name:	
Address:	
Phone:	
eMail:	
Notes:	

Date	Time	Service / Work	Price	Notes

Client Information

Name:	
Address:	
Phone:	
eMail:	
Notes:	

Date	Time	Service / Work	Price	Notes

Client Information

Name:	
Address:	
Phone:	
eMail:	
Notes:	

Date	Time	Service / Work	Price	Notes

Client Information

Name:	
Address:	
Phone:	
eMail:	
Notes:	

Date	Time	Service / Work	Price	Notes

Client Information

Name:	
Address:	
Phone:	
eMail:	
Notes:	

Date	Time	Service / Work	Price	Notes

Client Information

Name:	
Address:	
Phone:	
eMail:	
Notes:	

Date	Time	Service / Work	Price	Notes

Client Information

Name:	
Address:	
Phone:	
eMail:	
Notes:	

Date	Time	Service / Work	Price	Notes

Client Information

Name:	
Address:	
Phone:	
eMail:	
Notes:	

Date	Time	Service / Work	Price	Notes

Client Information

Name:	
Address:	
Phone:	
eMail:	
Notes:	

Date	Time	Service / Work	Price	Notes

Client Information

Name:	
Address:	
Phone:	
eMail:	
Notes:	

Date	Time	Service / Work	Price	Notes

Client Information

Name:	
Address:	
Phone:	
eMail:	
Notes:	

Date	Time	Service / Work	Price	Notes

Client Information

Name:	
Address:	
Phone:	
eMail:	
Notes:	

Date	Time	Service / Work	Price	Notes

Client Information

Name:	
Address:	
Phone:	
eMail:	
Notes:	

Date	Time	Service / Work	Price	Notes

Client Information

Name:	
Address:	
Phone:	
eMail:	
Notes:	

Date	Time	Service / Work	Price	Notes

Client Information

Name:	
Address:	
Phone:	
eMail:	
Notes:	

Date	Time	Service / Work	Price	Notes

Client Information

Name:	
Address:	
Phone:	
eMail:	
Notes:	

Date	Time	Service / Work	Price	Notes

Client Information

Name:	
Address:	
Phone:	
eMail:	
Notes:	

Date	Time	Service / Work	Price	Notes

Client Information

Name:	
Address:	
Phone:	
eMail:	
Notes:	

Date	Time	Service / Work	Price	Notes

Client Information

Name:	
Address:	
Phone:	
eMail:	
Notes:	

Date	Time	Service / Work	Price	Notes

Client Information

Name:	
Address:	
Phone:	
eMail:	
Notes:	

Date	Time	Service / Work	Price	Notes

Client Information

Name:	
Address:	
Phone:	
eMail:	
Notes:	

Date	Time	Service / Work	Price	Notes

Client Information

Name:	
Address:	
Phone:	
eMail:	
Notes:	

Date	Time	Service / Work	Price	Notes

Client Information

Name:	
Address:	
Phone:	
eMail:	
Notes:	

Date	Time	Service / Work	Price	Notes

Client Information

Name:	
Address:	
Phone:	
eMail:	
Notes:	

Date	Time	Service / Work	Price	Notes

Client Information

Name:	
Address:	
Phone:	
eMail:	
Notes:	

Date	Time	Service / Work	Price	Notes

Client Information

Name:	
Address:	
Phone:	
eMail:	
Notes:	

Date	Time	Service / Work	Price	Notes

Client Information

Name:	
Address:	
Phone:	
eMail:	
Notes:	

Date	Time	Service / Work	Price	Notes

Client Information

Name:	
Address:	
Phone:	
eMail:	
Notes:	

Date	Time	Service / Work	Price	Notes

Client Information

Name:	
Address:	
Phone:	
eMail:	
Notes:	

Date	Time	Service / Work	Price	Notes

Client Information

Name:	
Address:	
Phone:	
eMail:	
Notes:	

Date	Time	Service / Work	Price	Notes

Client Information

Name:	
Address:	
Phone:	
eMail:	
Notes:	

Date	Time	Service / Work	Price	Notes

Client Information

Name:	
Address:	
Phone:	
eMail:	
Notes:	

Date	Time	Service / Work	Price	Notes

Client Information

Name:	
Address:	
Phone:	
eMail:	
Notes:	

Date	Time	Service / Work	Price	Notes

Client Information

Name:	
Address:	
Phone:	
eMail:	
Notes:	

Date	Time	Service / Work	Price	Notes

Client Information

Name:	
Address:	
Phone:	
eMail:	
Notes:	

Date	Time	Service / Work	Price	Notes

Client Information

Name:	
Address:	
Phone:	
eMail:	
Notes:	

Date	Time	Service / Work	Price	Notes

Client Information

Name:	
Address:	
Phone:	
eMail:	
Notes:	

Date	Time	Service / Work	Price	Notes

Client Information

Name:	
Address:	
Phone:	
eMail:	
Notes:	

Date	Time	Service / Work	Price	Notes

Client Information

Name:	
Address:	
Phone:	
eMail:	
Notes:	

Date	Time	Service / Work	Price	Notes

Client Information

Name:	
Address:	
Phone:	
eMail:	
Notes:	

Date	Time	Service / Work	Price	Notes

Client Information

Name:	
Address:	
Phone:	
eMail:	
Notes:	

Date	Time	Service / Work	Price	Notes

Client Information

Name:	
Address:	
Phone:	
eMail:	
Notes:	

Date	Time	Service / Work	Price	Notes

Client Information

Name:	
Address:	
Phone:	
eMail:	
Notes:	

Date	Time	Service / Work	Price	Notes

Client Information

Name:	
Address:	
Phone:	
eMail:	
Notes:	

Date	Time	Service / Work	Price	Notes

Client Information

Name:	
Address:	
Phone:	
eMail:	
Notes:	

Date	Time	Service / Work	Price	Notes

Client Information

Name:	
Address:	
Phone:	
eMail:	
Notes:	

Date	Time	Service / Work	Price	Notes

Client Information

Name:	
Address:	
Phone:	
eMail:	
Notes:	

Date	Time	Service / Work	Price	Notes

Client Information

Name:	
Address:	
Phone:	
eMail:	
Notes:	

Date	Time	Service / Work	Price	Notes

Client Information

Name:	
Address:	
Phone:	
eMail:	
Notes:	

Date	Time	Service / Work	Price	Notes

Client Information

Name:	
Address:	
Phone:	
eMail:	
Notes:	

Date	Time	Service / Work	Price	Notes

Client Information

Name:	
Address:	
Phone:	
eMail:	
Notes:	

Date	Time	Service / Work	Price	Notes

Client Information

Name:	
Address:	
Phone:	
eMail:	
Notes:	

Date	Time	Service / Work	Price	Notes

Client Information

Name:	
Address:	
Phone:	
eMail:	
Notes:	

Date	Time	Service / Work	Price	Notes

Client Information

Name:	
Address:	
Phone:	
eMail:	
Notes:	

Date	Time	Service / Work	Price	Notes

Client Information

Name:	
Address:	
Phone:	
eMail:	
Notes:	

Date	Time	Service / Work	Price	Notes

Client Information

Name:	
Address:	
Phone:	
eMail:	
Notes:	

Date	Time	Service / Work	Price	Notes

Client Information

Name:	
Address:	
Phone:	
eMail:	
Notes:	

Date	Time	Service / Work	Price	Notes

Client Information

Name:	
Address:	
Phone:	
eMail:	
Notes:	

Date	Time	Service / Work	Price	Notes

Client Information

Name:	
Address:	
Phone:	
eMail:	
Notes:	

Date	Time	Service / Work	Price	Notes

Client Information

Name:	
Address:	
Phone:	
eMail:	
Notes:	

Date	Time	Service / Work	Price	Notes

Client Information

Name:	
Address:	
Phone:	
eMail:	
Notes:	

Date	Time	Service / Work	Price	Notes

Client Information

Name:	
Address:	
Phone:	
eMail:	
Notes:	

Date	Time	Service / Work	Price	Notes

Client Information

Name:	
Address:	
Phone:	
eMail:	
Notes:	

Date	Time	Service / Work	Price	Notes

Client Information

Name:	
Address:	
Phone:	
eMail:	
Notes:	

Date	Time	Service / Work	Price	Notes

Client Information

Name:	
Address:	
Phone:	
eMail:	
Notes:	

Date	Time	Service / Work	Price	Notes

Client Information

Name:	
Address:	
Phone:	
eMail:	
Notes:	

Date	Time	Service / Work	Price	Notes

Client Information

Name:	
Address:	
Phone:	
eMail:	
Notes:	

Date	Time	Service / Work	Price	Notes

Client Information

Name:	
Address:	
Phone:	
eMail:	
Notes:	

Date	Time	Service / Work	Price	Notes

Client Information

Name:	
Address:	
Phone:	
eMail:	
Notes:	

Date	Time	Service / Work	Price	Notes

Client Information

Name:	
Address:	
Phone:	
eMail:	
Notes:	

Date	Time	Service / Work	Price	Notes

Client Information

Name:	
Address:	
Phone:	
eMail:	
Notes:	

Date	Time	Service / Work	Price	Notes

Client Information

Name:	
Address:	
Phone:	
eMail:	
Notes:	

Date	Time	Service / Work	Price	Notes

Client Information

Name:	
Address:	
Phone:	
eMail:	
Notes:	

Date	Time	Service / Work	Price	Notes

Client Information

Name:	
Address:	
Phone:	
eMail:	
Notes:	

Date	Time	Service / Work	Price	Notes

Client Information

Name:	
Address:	
Phone:	
eMail:	
Notes:	

Date	Time	Service / Work	Price	Notes

Client Information

Name:	
Address:	
Phone:	
eMail:	
Notes:	

Date	Time	Service / Work	Price	Notes

Client Information

Name:	
Address:	
Phone:	
eMail:	
Notes:	

Date	Time	Service / Work	Price	Notes

Client Information

Name:	
Address:	
Phone:	
eMail:	
Notes:	

Date	Time	Service / Work	Price	Notes

Client Information

Name:	
Address:	
Phone:	
eMail:	
Notes:	

Date	Time	Service / Work	Price	Notes

Client Information

Name:	
Address:	
Phone:	
eMail:	
Notes:	

Date	Time	Service / Work	Price	Notes

www.ingramcontent.com/pod-product-compliance
Lightning Source LLC
Chambersburg PA
CBHW080555220526
45466CB00010B/3159
* 9 7 8 1 6 8 7 5 4 7 1 8 7 *